Red Leaf, Yellow Leaf

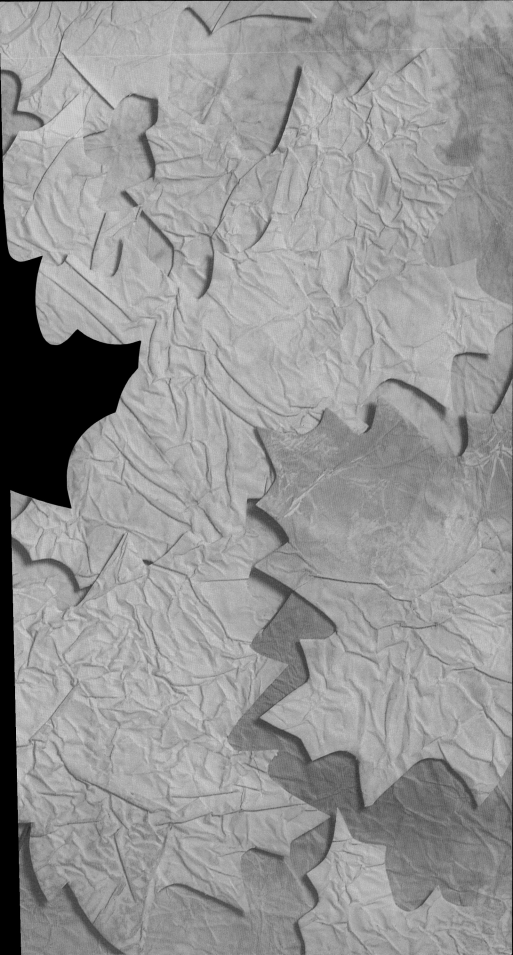

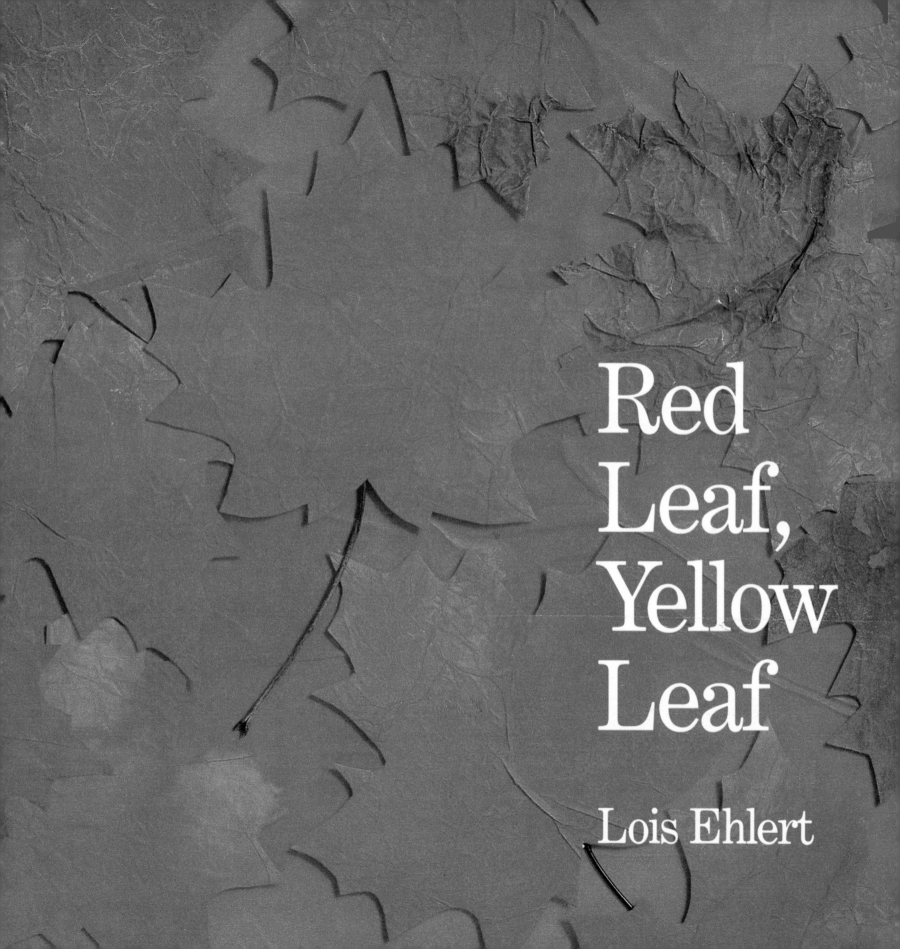

Red Leaf, Yellow Leaf

Lois Ehlert

Dedicated to our mothers' and fathers' trees and
especially to the trees we plant with our children

For AMJ, GE, HE, RMV, JHV, and PDJ

With special thanks to Beth Mittermaier, Al Stenstrup, Kathleen
Zuelsdorff, Havenwoods Environmental Center, Wehr Nature Center,
and Boerner Botanical Gardens, Milwaukee, Wisconsin

ISBN 0-590-46517-1

Copyright © 1991 by Lois Ehlert. All rights reserved. Published by Scholastic Inc.,
555 Broadway, New York, NY 10012, by arrangement with Harcourt Brace &
Company. SCHOLASTIC and associated logos are trademarks and/or registered
trademarks of Scholastic Inc.

12 11 10 9 8 7 6 5 4 3 2 1   9/9 0 1 2 3 4/0

Printed in the U.S.A.   08

First Scholastic paperback printing, September 1999

Author's Note

In the past, local nurseries got seedlings from the woods, as they do in this book,
but today they probably would order seedlings from a Pacific Northwest wholesale
tree supplier. The warm, wet weather there is perfect for growing trees. The
wholesale tree growers plant seeds and care for them. Until a tree is about four or
five feet tall, it is just a straight shoot with no side branches and is called a whip.
Growers pack these whips bare root (without soil) and ship them to local
nurseries, where they are transplanted and allowed to continue growing until
they are ready to deliver to garden centers.

first spring leaf

I've been saving this little leaf from my sugar maple tree so I could show it to you.
I love my tree.

It was born
long before I was.
The wind blew seeds
from the big maple trees
in the woods.
They twirled and whirled
as they fell to the ground.

Seeds the squirrels
didn't find lay sleeping
among the leaves

until they
were covered
with snow.

squirrel

maple tree seed

When spring sun warmed the seeds, they sprouted and sent roots down into the soil. Tiny leaves unfolded on their stems.

I think my tree would've been happy to stay there forever. But one day nursery workers came to the woods to collect tree sprouts.

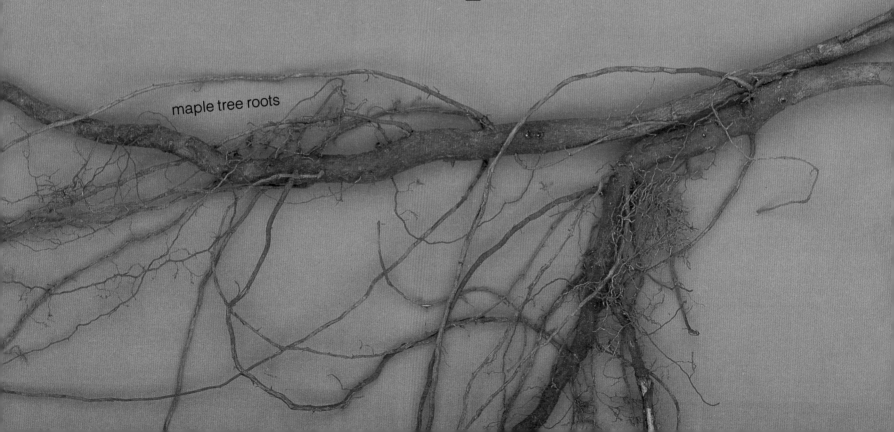

maple tree roots

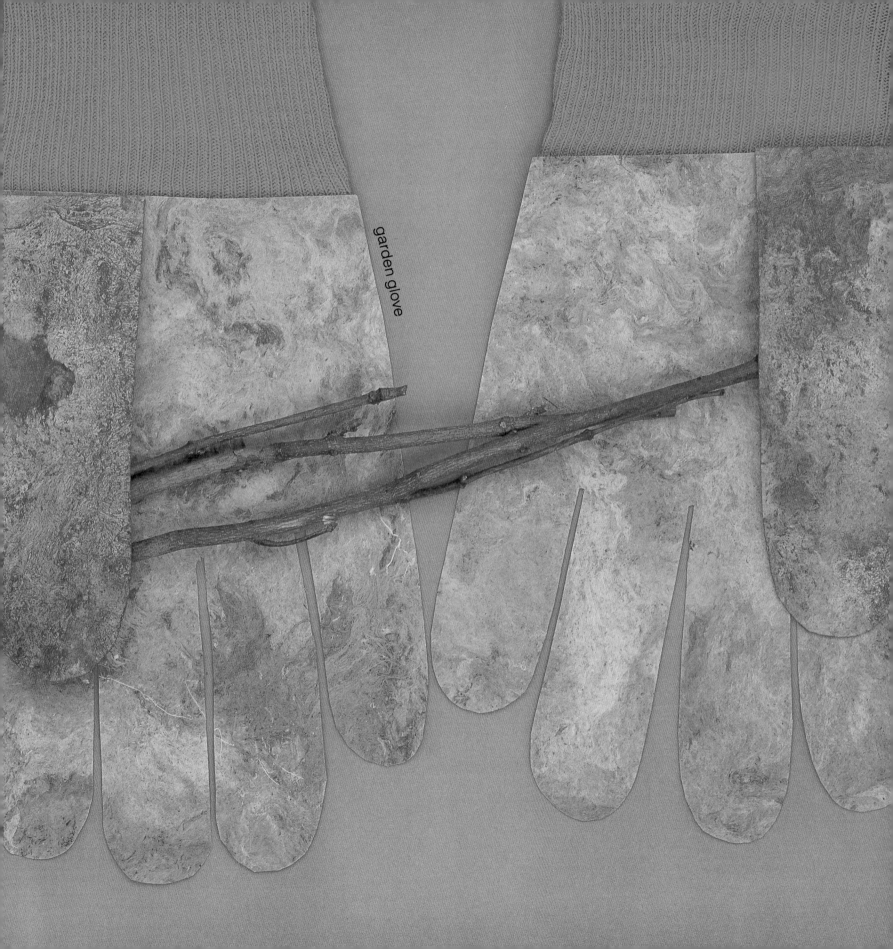

garden glove

Black-capped
Chickadee

They transplanted
the sprouts and tended
them year after year.

FALL DELIVERY / GARDEN CENTER

Just as the trees were settling in, they were measured, marked, and uprooted again!

Each ball of roots
was wrapped

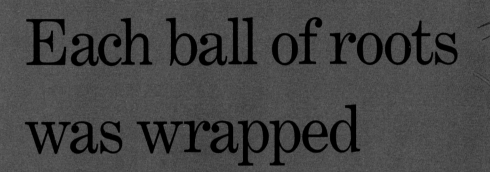

and tied
with twine.

Acer saccharum
SUGAR MAPLE

medium-growing pyramidal deciduous broad-leaved
tree — likes sun — height 30 to 40 feet — spread 15 to 20
feet — hardy to about −25°F

SUGAR
MAPLE

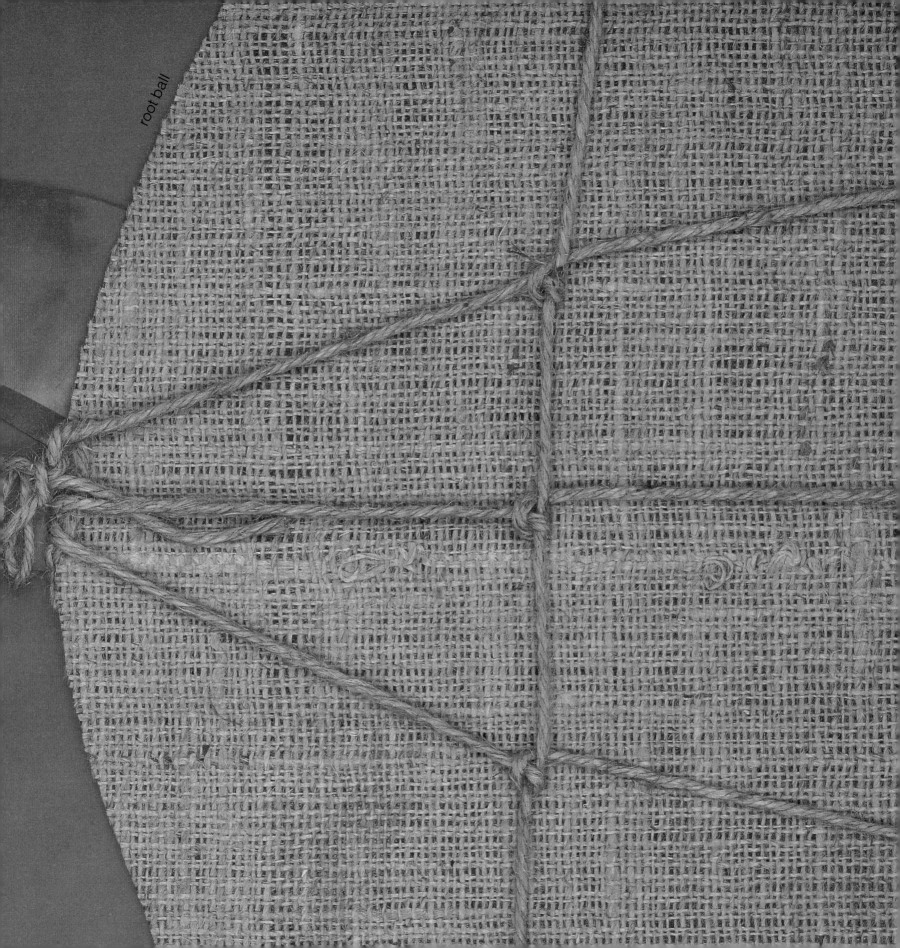
root ball

My tree was loaded onto a truck filled with other trees and delivered to the garden center.

delivery truck

WE ♥ TREES

Acer saccharum
SUGAR MAPLE
medium-growing pyramidal deciduous broad-leaved
tree — likes sun — height 30 to 40 feet — spread 15 to 20
feet — hardy to about −25°F

TRUCK

296

91 90

SUG
MA

We went there in the fall and picked out my tree.

SILVER MAPLE

NORWAY MAPLE

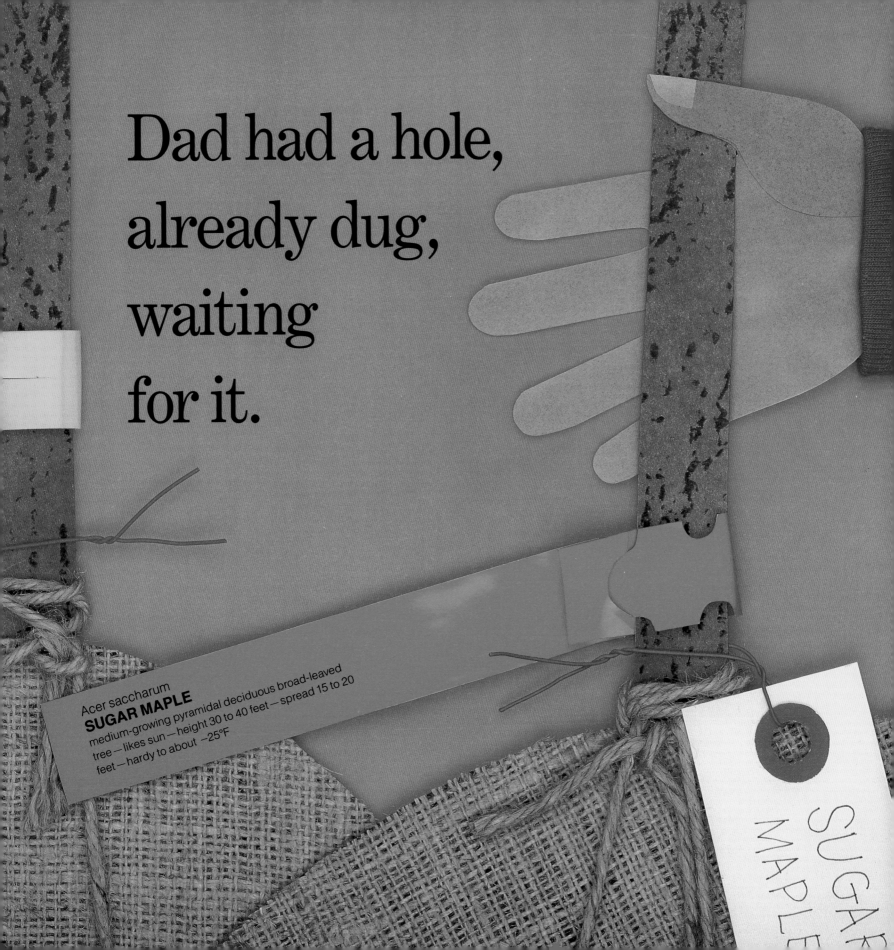

Dad had a hole, already dug, waiting for it.

Acer saccharum
SUGAR MAPLE
medium-growing pyramidal deciduous broad-leaved
tree—likes sun—height 30 to 40 feet—spread 15 to 20
feet—hardy to about −25°F

SUGAR
MAPLE

When we got home, we lowered my tree into the hole. I held the trunk while Dad covered the roots with soil.

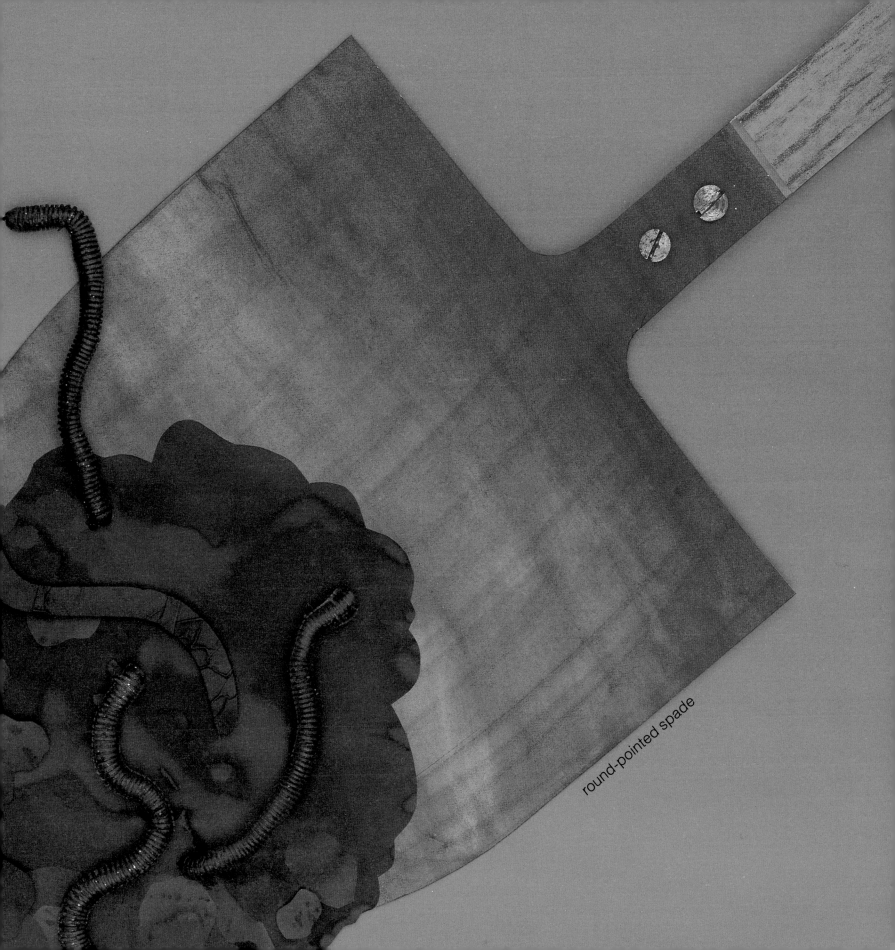

round-pointed spade

Now every
night before
I go to bed,
I peek out the
window and
wave to my tree.

bird treat

Downny Woodpecker

suet bag

bud

bird treat

When it
snows,
I hang up
treats for the birds.

maple tree
flowers

kite

young maple
tree leaves

Each spring,
I look for signs
that my tree is growing.

maple seeds

By late summer, the crown
of leaves is bushy and green.

paper
airplane

I love it when
the tree flowers turn
into winged seeds.

But if you want
to visit my tree,
come in the fall.

at's my favorite time.
Can you guess why?

Leaves

Leaves get their green color from a pigment called chlorophyll that helps them absorb sunlight. In a process called photosynthesis, leaves use water, energy from sunlight, and carbon dioxide from the air to make a type of sugar the tree needs for food. When leaves produce this sugar, they also give off oxygen, which purifies the air we breathe.

Maple leaves have other pigments, too. As days get shorter and temperatures cool down, the tree begins to rest. It stops making chlorophyll, and other pigments color the leaves red, orange, and yellow. This is a sign that the tree is getting ready for winter and will soon drop its leaves.

Buds

Buds on maple tree branches grow in pairs, one on each side of the stem. Some buds, usually the larger ones, grow into flowers, and others become leaves.

Roots and Sap

Roots are like underground branches that absorb minerals and water from the soil. The first root that the tree develops is called the taproot. As new roots grow, the taproot and older roots that grow out from it act as anchors so the tree doesn't tip over as it gets taller. The roots have root hairs along their sides, which feed the tree by absorbing nutrients such as water and minerals. The nutrients flow from the roots out to the branches through pipelike passages in the trunk. In early spring, while maple trees are still leafless and temperatures moderate, the sweet fluid called sap begins to run, feeding the tree buds. During this time a big maple tree, at least twelve inches in diameter, can be tapped without stressing the tree by drilling a hole in the bark and inserting a spout. Sap from the tree drips out through the hole. It is collected in a container and later boiled down to make maple syrup and sugar.

SUGAR MAPLE LEAF

Sugar maple bark

Bark

Bark is the outer skin of a tree. It protects the tree's interior from injury by animals and insects.

Tree Flowers

Maple trees bloom in the spring at about the same time that the leaves begin to appear. The flowers later become seeds.

Seeds

Maple tree seeds grow in winged seed cases called samaras, which develop out of the spring flowers. The seeds mature three or four months after the tree flowers fade. When the samaras drop off the trees, they spin on their wings and twirl as they fall to the ground. If they land in just the right spot, they will begin to grow. Each seed contains everything it needs to start a new tree. Birds, squirrels, and other small animals love to eat the seeds.

maple seeds (fall)

Selecting the Right Tree

Before going to the garden center, decide what kind of tree you want. You might see one you like as you take a walk or visit a park. You could also check seed catalogs or reference books at the library. Try to learn as much as you can about your tree before you bring it home. Consider where you will plant it and how large it will grow. Also be sure the tree you want will grow well in your climate and soil. If you pick a sugar maple like the one in this book, remember you might be the one who has to rake the red and yellow leaves in the fall.

Planting Times

The best time for planting trees is when they are dormant, or resting. This would be spring, before leaves develop, or fall, after the leaves drop off. These times are the least stressful for the tree, but trees can also be planted in summer if given plenty of water. Winter isn't usually suggested in cold areas where the ground freezes.

Preparing the Tree Site

You may want to dig a hole before you go to the garden center so it's ready for your tree when you bring it home. You will need to know approximately how big the root ball will be. Usually the hole should be twice as wide and one and a half times as deep as the root ball. While transplanting the tree, it is important to keep the roots moist at all times.

Planting
a Tree

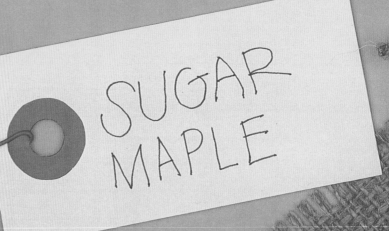

SUGAR MAPLE

Planting the Tree

After the hole is dug, put a mixture of peat moss and topsoil on the bottom. Add just enough so that when you put the root ball inside, its top will be level with the surrounding ground. A tree is heavier than it looks; it usually takes two adults to lift one. Pick up the tree by its root ball and gently lower it into the hole. Then cut the twine, loosen the burlap, and roll it back. Leave the burlap around the bottom of the root ball. It will decompose. Fill in the space around the root ball with soil, and make a ridge of soil around the edge of the hole. This ridge will help retain water near the tree's roots. Then water the tree thoroughly. You will need to continue to water your new tree regularly — sometimes twice a week in hot weather.

Wrapping

Wrapping the trunk of a new tree with burlap strips or tree tape protects its delicate bark from sun scald. It also prevents deer, rabbits, squirrels, and other animals from chewing the bark. You should leave the wrapping on for about two years.

Staking

If your tree trunk is larger than one inch in diameter, it needs to be supported with stakes so it won't tip over. Pound wooden stakes into the ground near the trunk and then tie them to the trunk with soft rope or burlap strips.

Red leaf,
Yellow leaf,
Beautiful tree.
Love,
from me